BY THE RIVER

by the river

Steven Herrick

FRONT STREET
Asheville, North Carolina

Originally published by Allen & Unwin, 2004

Printed in China
Designed by Helen Robinson
First U.S. edition
Second printing

Library of Congress Cataloging-in-Publication Data

Herrick, Steven.
  By the river / Steven Herrick.— 1st U.S. ed.
      p. cm.
Summary: A fourteen-year-old describes, through prose poems, his life
in a small Australian town in 1962, where, since their mother's death, he
and his brother have been mainly on their own to learn about life, death,
and love.
ISBN-13: 978-1-932425-72-7
ISBN-10: 1-932425-72-1 (alk. paper)
[1. Brothers—Fiction. 2. Single-parent families—Fiction.
3. Fathers and sons—Fiction. 4. Death—Fiction.
5. Australia—Fiction.] I. Title.

PZ7.H43214By 2006
[Fic]—dc22

2005023967

FRONT STREET
An Imprint of Boyds Mills Press, Inc.
A Highlights Company
815 Church Street
Honesdale, Pennsylvania 18431

Dedicated to my brothers:
Denis, Ray, Les
and in memory, Johnny

THE COLOR OF MY TOWN

THE COLOR OF MY TOWN

Red
was Johnny Barlow
with his lightning fists
that drew blood in a blur.
Yellow
was Urger,
who stood behind,
with crooked teeth,
spitting and cursing.
Blue
were Miss Spencer's eyes,
pale and shining,
and fading distant gray
as the taxi drove away.
Green
was my dad's handkerchief,
ironed,
pressed into the pocket
above his heart;
a box of handkerchiefs
Mum gave him on his birthday
two weeks before she died.
Brown
was dry grass all summer,
a dead snake,

cane toads squashed flat,

our house smeared in oil;

nothing that lives,

nothing that shines.

White

was Mum's nightgown,

the chalk Miss Carter used

to write my name,

hospital sheets,

and the color of Linda's cross.

ONE HARRY

THE SCRAPHEAP

My dad
wore a blue singlet,
khaki shorts,
and Army socks rolled down
over steel-capped boots.
His legs
were muscle brown
from riding his old pushbike
three miles to work and back
at Deakin Foundry.
There he wore
goggles
and a mask
as he fed sheet-metal
into the grinder,
and little iron filings
would spray his skin
with needle-point accuracy,
"so sharp it was like
getting tattooed
every day
for twenty years."
Each afternoon
he'd sit with
my brother Keith

and me

in the backyard,

down by the chook shed,

with a watermelon

and a carving knife.

He'd slice chunks

bigger than my face

and we'd eat,

spitting the pips

to the chickens

and laughing at the pink juice

dribbling down onto the grass.

We'd toss the rind

into the scrapheap

behind the shed

where the chickens

spent all day searching.

One day

Keith saw a brown snake

slide into the heap.

We ran to get Dad

and he came down

with two shovels,

"one for trapping firm,

one for chopping."

He had Wellington boots

knee high,

in case the snake
struck first,
but no snake
was as fast
as my dad.

OIL FOR PAINT

We lived
in a weathered timber cottage
that Dad refused to paint.
He got Keith and me
to brush sump oil
onto the hardwood walls.
The house looked
brown, shabby
and mean
and everyone loved
giving directions to the
Hodby house.
"Just look for the house
smeared in oil,"
they'd say.
"Down Keeling Street.
You'll see it.
Or smell it."
They liked to spit
things like that,
the men at Chardons Pub,
the ladies at Evans' Grocery.
I once got into a fight
with Craig Randall
over

the Hodby house

and what he said,

even though

I agreed with every word.

I ended up

with a bloody nose

and a swollen lip

defending

the house

that stained my fingers

and my heart.

SIX YEARS OLD

I could cook
at the age of seven.
My dad taught me—
eggs,
steak,
vegetables,
rice,
and roast chicken—
in our old oven
with the door so heavy
and hot
it burnt my fingers
four times
before I learned
how to push and turn,
holding the tea towel tight.
My brother, Keith,
could sweep
the cottage in ten minutes flat,
and he kept the bathroom
shining like a medal.
Keith and me joked
about our neat
clean home
that looked dirt-poor

from the street
but smelt of chicken roast
and disinfectant inside,
where my brother
and me shared
the duties
our mother left us.
She died
when I was seven,
and Keith was
six years old.

THE WHIRLIGIG

It's Keith's
birthday present.
We place Dad's ladder
against the house
and first me,
then Keith,
climb onto the roof,
dragging our weight
over the rusted gutters
onto the corrugated iron.
We scramble
up to the pitch
and sit
looking across town
down to the creek.
Keith holds the whirligig
in one hand
and pulls the cord
with the other,
and we watch
that birthday present
soar, spinning wildly,
over the Spencer house,
clear across Cowpers Paddock,
to crash somewhere

this side of Durra Creek.

Keith and me

look at each other,

laugh,

slide down the roof

to the ladder

and race

to find the whirligig

and do it all again,

until Dad gets home

and the watermelon calls.

SUNDAY MORNING

The first Sunday
of every month,
my dad,
Keith, and me
put on clean clothes
and us boys
wear shoes
for the only time
that week.
We walk across town to
Oakwood Cemetery
at a bend in the big river
where a truck driver lost brakes
and hope,
and they buried him
near Mum's grave
with the mud-slow water
rolling past.
Keith and me
pick fresh daisies,
blooms for Mum's headstone,
while Dad
pulls weeds
and sweeps clean
the marble

with wild grass stalks.
We sit in the
tender shade
of an old casuarina.
My dad flicks some coins
to Keith and me
for chips
from the shop
across the way,
and
we leave him
to share some time
with our mother,
his wife.

ON A LOG IN COWPERS PADDOCK

After school
we stop at Cowpers Paddock
and look for field mice.
We sit on a log
watching the hawk
wheel above,
a targeting arc,
till his wings fold
into a glorious dive.
Keith and me
dream of nets
strung across,
released on cue
to catch hawk
and mouse,
for no reason other
than one can fly
and one can hide,
while
Keith and me
can do neither,
sitting,
easy prey,
on a log in Cowpers Paddock
in our small town.

THE WITCHES OF WILLIAM STREET

Keith and me

throw rocks from the footpath

onto the tin roof

of the house draped in creepers,

while the witches of William Street

stand on the verandah

waving their arms

as we sprint away.

Lightning flashes, thunder cracks.

I'd swear there was a broom

by the front door,

tanked up,

ready to chase us down the street

with a witch aboard.

We hide at Cowpers Paddock

until the storm comes,

the storm summoned by those

spider-haired demons

the neighborhood calls

the Clarke sisters

who, legend has it,

never married, and buried

their father's fortune

under the house.

There they sit,

holding the world at bay

until the Hodby kids,

bound to turn out bad,

attack with an artillery fire

of pebbles exploding on the roof.

They shout a curse,

only to see the

hasty retreat

of two schoolboys

convinced they are

saving their town

from enemy invasion;

two running heroes

waving

from the front page

of their imagination.

THE CAKE

Linda Mahony
had knocked quietly,
so quiet I didn't hear,
but I knew.
I opened the door.
Linda said,
"Hello, Harry.
My mum said to bring this over.
To say we're sorry."
She held out an orange cake
and a card.
"I drew a picture in the card
for you, and Keith."
I stood holding the cake,
looking at Linda's drawing
of my mum
in heaven, with God,
and the angels,
all in pink and blue crayon.
Linda waved from the gate
and walked down Keeling Street,
the sun on her green dress
and her long dark hair.
I'd never tasted
a cake so sweet and delicious.

For two nights,
after dinner,
it took me away
from Mum,
gone a week,
and Dad,
alone in the kitchen,
stirring his tea
until it was cold in the cup;
stirring, around and around,
while
I ate two helpings
of Linda's cake,
seven years and four days
before she died
in the flood.

MRS. APPLEYARD

Mrs. Appleyard

says us boys

need a mum

because our clothes

look old as rags

and are twice as dirty.

Mrs. Appleyard

says we stay up

way too late

and shout like demons

in the backyard,

enough so her hens can't lay.

Mrs. Appleyard

says the Department should know,

and find us a real home,

with a mother there

when we get home from school.

Mrs. Appleyard says

a man can't bring up children alone.

Mrs. Appleyard.

Mrs. Appleyard.

Go and get stuffed.

THE BIG RIVER

The big river
rolls past our town
at Hobsons Bend,
takes a slow look
at the houses on stilts
with timber creaking, paint flaking,
at the graveyard hushed
in the lonely shade,
at the fruit bats
dropping mango pulp
into the undergrowth,
at the foundry, and sawmill
grinding under a blazing sun,
at the pub with welcoming verandahs
shaded in wisteria vine,
at Durra Creek surrendering
to the incessant flow,
at Pearce Swamp upstream
on the creek among the willows
and rivergums,
at the storm clouds
rumbling over Rookwood Hill,
at the two boys
casting a line
on the crumbling bank,

at the cow fields
purple with Paterson's curse,
at the jammed tree trunks
washed down after summer thunder,
at the shop
with dead flies in the window display,
at the mosquito mangroves
and the sucking sound of mud crabs,
at the children throwing mulberries
that stain like lipstick.
The big river
rolls past our town,
takes a slow look,
and rolls away.

AUNT ALICE

Too old
for marriage
and nonsense,
she brings lamingtons
on Wednesday afternoon,
wearing
her gray woollen dress
with a shawl of black,
even in summer,
and her felt hat
always tilted
slightly to the left.
She knocks
and walks in,
talking all the time
of us boys
with no shoes
and hair never combed.
She grabs Keith
by the ear,
feigns disgust,
and sends us both
to the bathroom
with washing orders,
"No cakes for the unclean."

She boils the kettle,
sets the table
with a white cloth
she's brought with her,
and we sit,
a lamington on each plate,
waiting
for Dad to arrive home.
Me and Keith,
our eyes fixed on the cake,
pray
that Dad hasn't stopped
at Chardons Pub
or Evans' Grocery,
or anywhere
that keeps us
another minute
from Aunt Alice's treats.

ESCAPE ARTIST

"You can get out of anything
with that mouth of yours."
Miss Carter
sent me back
to my chair,
and I kept my head down
all afternoon,
not wanting
to push my luck.
Her gray hair
bristled
as she wielded the ruler,
like my dad worked an axe.
Thirty-two years
at the one school
gave her an eagle's authority
and a snake's bite.
My dad named me
Harry,
after Harry Houdini,
who could escape
from boxes locked with chains,
under water,
and who went over waterfalls
in wooden barrels

and walked away.

In class

I proved my name

was well chosen,

with a careful word,

or an innocent silence

that left Miss Carter

gripping the long ruler

and smacking it

against the chalkboard,

her eyes never leaving me.

Harry.

Harry Hodby.

THE PIEMAN

The pieman
came to our school
every day at lunchtime.
He parked his van
on the footpath,
loaded his oven
with split firewood
and waited.
I could taste the hardwood smoke
in each pie.
Keith and me would sit
under the fig tree
and eat two pies each.
Our dad's treat for Monday only,
but one day
the pieman
heaped too much wood,
still damp,
into the oven.
Two hundred children
stood at the fence
watching the van,
smoke black and pungent,
while the pieman swore and shouted
and swore some more,

until the cleaner
soaked the van
with the school hose,
and Keith and me
thought of the useless coins
jangling in our pockets.
Our stomachs rumbled
while the pieman sat in the gutter
swearing
at the blackened shell
of his work gone bad.

GAMES

Linda had brown eyes
that danced
through each lesson.
In class
we'd play
our secret game called,
"wink when wrong."
She'd sit two rows
away from me
as Miss Carter started
"Monday 20 Questions,"
which we all hated.
Every time someone
answered wrong
Linda would wink
her left eye at me.
She'd never raise her hand
to volunteer the correct answer.
"The capital of Switzerland?"
"The longest river in the world?"
It was much more fun
to watch Miss Carter
growing redder
as Scuzz answered,
"The capital of Switzerland is S, Miss.

And the longest river is the Pacific, Miss."
All morning
I sat back,
content to watch Linda
with her brown eyes,
playing games.

THE HAIRCUT

Aunt Alice arrives, as usual,

with lamingtons and demands

to "clean this, tidy that."

But today

she carries scissors,

and we know her intention.

Keith sits on the back stairs

with a dessert bowl

on his head,

eyes closed,

and Aunt Alice

cutting,

swift as an executioner,

every hair that falls lower

than the bowl.

"Finished!"

Keith walks inside

like a defeated soldier

with his helmet still on.

"Harry. Next."

I fake injury,

lice,

dizzy spells,

but Aunt Alice

can't be fooled.

I sit on the stairs,

eyes shut,

listening to the clip clip

of scissors

but only hearing

the laughter and shouts

tomorrow at school

of

"Helmet-head Hodby!"

firing across the battlefield

we call a playground.

"Helmet-head Hodby!"

EGGS

Early on Saturday,
Dad collects the eggs
from our chook shed.
He keeps a dozen.
The rest he packs
in an old shoebox.
He calls Keith
or me,
and asks us to take them
to Mr. Ross next door,
or the Spencers,
or Mrs. Appleyard.
Once, I pleaded,
"No, Dad, not her.
She's always going on
about me and Keith . . .
And she's got her own hens."
Dad smiled and said,
"Better to be friends
with neighbors, Harry.
Mrs. Appleyard has her moments."
So I trudged down Keeling Street.
And what did she say
as she took our eggs?
"Well. It's the least you can do.

All that noise you make
has stopped my hens from laying.
Thank your father for me, young man."

I walked home,
saying to myself,
"Your hens aren't laying
because they're as old as *you*,
Mrs. Appleyard!"

ROMANCE?

"Are you dreaming,
Linda Mahony?
On holiday already?
Or perhaps off with a boyfriend?"
Miss Carter tapped the chalkboard
as Linda blushed
and all the girls giggled nervously,
waiting for another lecture
on the evils of romance,
and where it leads.
"Time enough for romance
when you're older, Linda.
Study now, dream later,
I always say."
Linda blushed again.
Scuzz made kissing noises.
Red yelled, "Oh yuk!"
I wanted to punch Scuzz,
and Red,
but instead
I raised my hand,
and said,
"How come you never married,
Miss Carter?"

STORIES

Linda and me were friends.
Good friends.
Sometimes,
after school,
we'd sit in the crook
of the fig tree
and she'd read aloud
the stories
she wrote late at night
when her family slept.
Stories about rafting,
or swimming,
or riding surfboards
on a sparkling beach
somewhere in the future.
And she drew
pictures of herself
standing on a stage
holding a trophy.
One was called,
"Queen of the Surf."
I sat in the shade,
enjoying her dreams
and the sound of her eager voice
until she'd stop,

close her book,

look up at me

and ask,

"What do you want to be, Harry?"

TWO · A PATCH OF DAISIES

A PATCH OF DAISIES

In 1962
I was fourteen,
and the flood swept
refrigerators, bikes,
used tires, and
Linda Mahony
downstream.
A gang of boys
searched the creek
at Freemans Bush
for treasure,
or Linda.
Days later,
they found her.
Two kids fishing
at Pearce Swamp
for yabbies.
In a ghost of bubbles,
Linda rose
from under a jam of logs.
Her body,
full of creek water,
weeds,
and thirteen years' memory,
popped out of the swamp

like a cork held down too long
and scared the boys
into nightmares.
They never went fishing again
at that place
where the willows weep.
The Mahony family
moved south,
after planting
a white cross
and a patch of daisies
that sometimes,
when the day was too hot
for homework,
I'd weed
so that our town
had something
worth remembering.

ROOKWOOD HILL

Keith and me work
for weeks on the billycart.
Pram wheels found at the dump,
a fruit box from the grocery,
nails and timber from under the house,
and a leather strap
Dad brought home from the foundry.
On Saturday morning
Dad gets his oilcan,
soaks the axle and wheels,
checks the strap is nailed firm.
The circle of leather stretches from
the front axle to the fruit box,
where Keith sits holding the reins
of our timber horse.
Dad wishes us good luck
and we walk a mile
to Rookwood Hill,
climb slowly
up the gravel incline
and stand at the top
looking over the fields below.
The track looks bumpy, hard,
with potholes all the way down
and a sharp left turn at the bottom,

or else you'd fly straight into the lantana bush.
We stand on Rookwood Hill,
the billycart between us,
both thinking,
"A brake. We forgot a brake."
Keith hands me the reins,
smirks, and says,
"You first. You're the eldest."
I take the strap,
sit in the cart,
close my eyes,
and push off . . .

That's how I got this scar
five inches long on my leg:
a billycart,
no brake,
a lantana bush,
and Rookwood Hill.

UNDER LAMPLIGHT

Dad bathes the wound
with warm water,
dabbing lightly at the deep cut
still oozing blood.
He gently places yellow gauze
across the gash,
and wraps a bandage, tight.
He holds my leg high
as I sit on the lounge,
and places pillows under the heel,
"so the blood runs to your brain,
not on the floor."
That night in bed
I wake when I turn.
I see Dad
sitting in the corner of my room
reading a book under lamplight.
All night, awake,
in case his son,
who can't turn a corner on a billycart,
needs him.

THE SUMMER HEAT

No one swam
at Pearce Swamp,
not since Linda died.
Scuzz
got his dad's
bolt-cutters
and cut a hole, body-size,
in the western fence
of the Army Reserve.
We climbed through,
towels and swimmers ready,
and ran to the pit,
full from summer storms.
Our new swimming hole.
Rumor spread:
the Army dumped disused weapons
and unexploded shells
into the pit,
and sometimes
we saw dark shadows
below.
And once
Scuzz got chased to the bank
by a red-bellied black snake.
The gang spent every weekend there

because
bombs
and guns
and snakes
were harmless shapes
beside the ghost of Linda
guarding Pearce Swamp
in the afternoon heat.

ALWAYS BAD NEWS

First
they jab our arms.
Six little punctures
to test whether or not
we need the big needle.
We sit together
during lunch
watching
the red marks rise,
or disappear,
not knowing
which is good news
or bad.
Johnny Barlow
scoffs at our worries.
"Like a cop knocking
on your door
late at night,
it's always bad news."
This afternoon
I stand behind Johnny
in line,
watching
as he looks away.
The needle is

like a pistol,
aimed dead square
at his shoulder.
I see his teeth clench
and his jaw go tight,
then he turns to me,
"It's always bad news,
Hodby,
always bad."
He cocks his fingers
and points
the gun my way
as I step forward,
close my eyes,
and wait for
the policeman's knock.

MY DAD, AND THE DRUNK SILENCED

His knuckles
are blood-stained,
swollen
like four tear-shaped tattoos.
He sits at the dinner table
eating,
his left hand
shovelling the fork,
his right hand
in a bowl
of Dettol water,
warm,
"to wash away
Old Man Barlow's germs."
After dinner,
without a word,
he gives Keith
a pound note—
a fresh pound note,
so crisp it crackles
when Keith puts it
into his pocket.
Keith runs to the shop,
and comes back
with

two all-day suckers
for him and me,
and a bottle of beer
for Dad
to forget
the drunk's words
flung around the pub
about us no-good boys.

HUMBUG

On the oval
at lunchtime,
Johnny Barlow
walks up to me.
I clench my fist
and think of
Dad's knuckles—
swollen.
Johnny is two months
and six inches
bigger than me,
and his teeth
are as crooked
as his family.
His hair is cut
razor short,
and he has big ears
that hear insults
whispered
a classroom away.
Johnny Barlow
walks up to me,
stands close,
too close,
and says,

"Your dad,
he's a good fighter."
Then he shakes my hand
and walks away
and I feel
the Humbug lolly
he's left in my palm.
I slip it
into my pocket,
unsure
whether to thank
Johnny,
or my dad.

THE TOWN DOG

The dog crosses the train tracks,
head down, tongue out,
a limp in one leg.
It sniffs the stinkweed
beside the tracks,
cocks a leg
and stains its territory.
I can hear horse races
from a scratchy radio
as I sit after school
on a tired swing
in Devitt Park.
The dog sees me
and barks once.
I hold out my hand
and he comes in close,
wary,
until I click my fingers
and encourage him.
I rub behind his ears,
and pat his sides.
I have a friend
here
in this solitary park,
as I wait

for my dad
to come home
on a balmy afternoon.

TWENTY AT A TIME

"Butterflies,
millions of them
at Cowpers Paddock!"
A gang of us
run down,
wonder fast.
We stand statue
at the sight
of yellows, whites,
brown-blacks
and feather-grays,
floating on
the east wind
across acres of waving grass.
Then, with arms wide,
we walk
like apostles
through the gates of heaven
into the gossamer mist.
They brush our hair and
caress our faces.
One gray lands on
my wrist
and stays there
as I walk him

through

this rainbow wind,

until

Peter Evans

comes down to the paddock

swinging his

new tennis racket,

killing twenty butterflies

at a time

with each forehand smash.

THE VALUE OF PROPERTY

Keith,
Johnny Barlow,
and me
are given
punishment
of one week each,
sweeping
Evans' Grocery
every afternoon,
to pay for
the tennis racket
we thumped over a log
at Cowpers Paddock
until it was as twisted
as Peter,
who ran home crying.
And because
he wears shoes
and clean clothes,
and has his hair
neatly parted
straight-down-the-middle;
and because Keith and me
live in a house
smeared in oil,

without a mother;

and because

Johnny's eldest brother is

serving time in

Millthorpe Prison;

everyone

sides with Peter

and decides to teach us

the value of property.

So Keith,

Johnny Barlow,

and me

sweep and mop

and dust

and learn the

value of property,

each slipping an

all-day sucker

into our pocket

when Mr. Evans

isn't watching.

NOTHING TO EARN

The next day,
while emptying scraps
onto the heap,
I notice
the wattlebirds
in the bottlebrush
along the fence.
They sit, sentry,
in the high branches,
until one bird
makes that scrapping,
jagged screech,
and then they all start.
I stand holding the bin,
lost in this orchestra
playing only for me
and the scrapheap,
while
Peter Evans
is getting fat
on the lollies
and ginger beer
and chips
he does nothing to earn.

THE FLOOD

At Linda's cross,
I sit on a log
and listen
to the sound of
a distant freight train
leaving town.
I watch the lazy clouds
drift their shadows
across the surface
of the swamp.
I feel bad I'm the only one
willing to come here
to remember Linda
and the day of the flood,
when the big river
burst its banks
and poured into the flatlands
near Durra Creek
and swept
so much of the town
into crazy whirlpools
that circled the willows
down here
at Pearce Swamp.

LINDA

She was my friend
because
the day after I fought
Craig Randall
over what he said
about my house,
Linda came to school
with my favorite orange cake—
two slices—
and we shared at lunch
under the fig tree.
She let me read
her new story:
about a house
painted dull brown
that everyone in town
laughed at.
And one day
crowds gathered
outside the house
to poke fun
at the family
who stood, defiant,
in the front yard,
when, suddenly,
a storm came

from the west.
But no one left
to escape the downpour
because
before their very eyes
the rain washed away
the brown paint
to reveal a house
coated in gold,
glistening
like a palace.
And the yard
was transformed
into colorful flowerbeds
of roses and daisies,
and the trees
grew heavy with fruit—
peaches, apples, and
the sweetest mulberries.
And as the rain cleared,
the family,
who everyone had laughed at,
picked the fruit,
and, without saying a word,
handed it across
the fence
to the townsfolk.

ON GUARD

They say
Birdy Newman
lost his mind
in the war
and spends his days
looking for it
in Freemans Bush,
where he lives in a tent,
and late at night
he roams the forest
with a double-edged knife
and fishing rope,
in case the Japanese
invade.
Sometimes
we see him
by Hobsons Bend.
We shout, "Hey, Birdy."
He waves and grins,
then puts his finger to his lips
so we stay quiet
"in case the enemy hears."
He's called
Birdy
because he has the

flashing eyes

of a sparrow.

My dad

says Birdy's lived his life

in the cross hairs,

waiting for the trigger.

Every Christmas,

Dad buys some beer,

disappears into the forest,

and doesn't come back until late.

When Keith asks him,

Dad laughs

and says,

"Birdy deserves a beer.

After all,

no one's invaded

since he's been

on guard."

CLIMBING TREES

Oaks,
firs,
even Moreton Bay figs.
You grip
and swing your feet,
pull,
then it's like
climbing
a scratchy ladder
until
you're hidden by leaves.
And for hours,
if you're quiet,
people
walk by
talking of
shopping,
and husbands,
money,
and death,
and who got drunk
last Saturday
and slept on the front lawn
for all the world to see.
My town

tells me its mysteries
as I sit
silent
thirty foot in the sky.

FOR A LONG TIME

It's cool here
in the shade,
high in my favorite oak,
listening to the wind
and Mrs. Appleyard
both blowing hard
through our small town.
I lean back
and remember
the stories Linda
would share,
and her eyes
sparkling.
"What do you want to be, Harry?"

Mrs. Appleyard
spits gossip
on Birdy and his madness,
and
Old Man Barlow's latest binge,
and
those boys running wild
through Cowpers Paddock
chasing whirligigs
and butterflies . . .

Linda,
I want to learn enough
to find the quickest way out,
and I promise
when I leave
I won't come back,
not for a long time.

THE DAWSON GYM

The gym
is an old shed
that smells of liniment,
sweat, and Bert Dawson's pipe.
I sit on the hardwood bench
along the back wall,
watching
the boxers work on weights,
or rock the bag
with eighty hits per minute,
as Dawson shouts abuse,
his pipe bouncing
onto the sawdust-covered floor.
On Saturdays
he charges
threepence admission
to watch
his charges go two rounds each.
Me and Keith
sit up the back
and flinch
as kids, our age,
walk into haymakers
that send them sprawling to the canvas,
with Dawson ringing the bell

while the men
in the front row holler.
One day I saw Johnny Barlow
knock down
a boy two years older
and a foot taller,
with a left hook
that sounded like a hammer
hitting soft wood.
The boy stayed down.
Johnny stood
and looked out at the crowd.
He saw me and Keith
and I swear he winked
and smacked one killer glove
into the other.
Keith cheered and waved.
I looked away.

BECAUSE I CAN

Keith, Johnny, and me
walk home from the gym
cutting across Cowpers Paddock,
remembering butterflies
and the colorful wind.
"Like walking through heaven," I say.
"Better than holidays,
better than swimming,
better than boxing," says Johnny.
Keith looks at me, then Johnny,
and asks,
"Why do you do it?"
Johnny kicks a rock,
shields his eyes from the sun
as he looks across at us,
and says, "Because I can.
Because my dad says so.
Because I've got nothing better to do.
Have you?"
Keith shrugs an answer.
I want to say,
"Yeah, Johnny.
Anything's better than
getting punched
or punching somebody."
But I don't.

HALF-A-MILE HIGH

Keith and me
wake before sunrise,
pack our bags with lunch,
leave a note for Dad,
and start on our long ride.
There isn't a headwind,
so we cycle, nonstop
for three hours,
to reach Red Cliffs Airport.
We leave our bikes
near the scribbly gums,
climb the fence,
and creep slowly
to the end of the runway.
There we lie on our backs,
hidden under some bushes,
and watch as the planes
shoot over our heads,
fifty yards straight up:
so close we can read
their call-numbers,
see the tread in each tire,
and hear the whine
of the engines cruising in.
We sit there for hours,

watching the planes
take off and land,
and dreaming of one day
strapping ourselves in,
and flying back home
to wave at our schoolmates
as we buzz along
half-a-mile high.

THE DRAGON SLAYER

My window glows orange.
I wake to sounds
of cracking glass
and shouting voices.
I shove Keith awake
and we run outside
where Dad
and Mr. Ross
are breaking down
the door of the Kerry house.
Dad's axe swings
time and again
until the door splinters
and the flame
leaps out at the men
like a caged dragon
released.
They fight back
with blankets soaked in water.
Dad disappears inside.
Keith and me stand at our gate.
The fibro splits
and cracks
as the dragon breaks
the house's back.

The walls collapse

while Mr. Ross

waters the beast

with a limp garden hose.

The smoke gets thicker

and blacker and deadlier.

I start to pray

for the first time in years,

trying desperately to remember the words,

as Keith shouts for Dad

and the fire rages.

Dad drags Mr. Kerry—

still holding his bottle—

into the front yard.

Mr. Ross

trains his hose

on the drunk,

and my dad—

the dragon slayer.

LEAVING

For a month
after the fire
I wake
to hear Dad
coughing
late into the night.
Sometimes
I go to the kitchen,
fill a glass,
and take it
into his room.
In the dark
he whispers thanks.
I go back to bed
thinking of Mr. Kerry
in an ambulance
and the talk
of him in a Home
for drunks and madmen,
miles from here.
As the branches
scrape their fingers
down my window,
and the clock ticks slowly
in the hallway,

I lie awake
thinking how
people leave this town:
in an ambulance,
or worse . . .

MEASURE

They put a tape
across the fence
to keep us out of the ruins
of the Kerry house.
We step over it
and explore.
Grass and weeds
as high as the fence.
Shattered glass in the house,
and the iron bed, blackened,
where Old Man Kerry slept
as Dad risked his life.
I stand in the hallway,
between the broken walls,
and marvel at how little
is left:
the kitchen sink,
the toilet,
and a backyard full
of empty beer bottles
to measure
Mr. Kerry's life.

SLUMBER

In summer
I walk to Rookwood Hill
and climb the cedar tree.
From the highest branch
I can see
across the flatlands
to the far side of town
where Durra Creek
flows into the big river
at Hobsons Bend.
The clear waters
of the creek
dissolve in the marsh brown
and gather speed
as the river
turns its back
on the town
and rolls south.
I trace Durra Creek
back across the fields
to Pearce Swamp
hidden amongst
a stand of red gums and willows.
Bellbirds ring across the plain.
Cicadas echo from every tree:

a deafening rhythm
as I watch my town
slumber
in the suffocating heat.

BIG NIGHT OUT

On Friday nights
I cook sausages
for Keith and me.
We have sandwiches
smeared in tomato sauce,
with a sausage rolled between.
Friday is Dad's pub night.
He sits at the bar
with a beer,
and some hot chips
soaked in vinegar.
Sometimes he plays darts,
or listens to the greyhound races
on the radio,
as men all around him
tear up losing tickets,
while Dad
eats another chip,
takes a swig of beer,
and tries his best
to enjoy
his big night out.

COLD-BLOODED ANIMALS

At Linda's cross—
with heat bubbles rising
from Pearce Swamp
and the lizards
on half-submerged logs,
tails splashing
in the calm water—
I find a silver ring
with sapphire glass.
It's by the cross,
as if someone
has knelt here,
said a prayer,
with only the lizards
and the swamp,
and maybe Linda,
to hear.
I can see footprints
near the daisies.
I try the ring on,
feel a shiver
as it slips neatly
onto my smallest finger.
I pull it off,
look around,

afraid I'm being watched.
I place the ring
back near the cross
and leave the swamp
to cold-blooded animals
and the barefoot ghost.

THREE LOVE AND SEX

NUMB

Late Friday,
after Dad is home
and snoring,
Keith and me climb out
our window
and shadow-quiet
creep to Dylan Street
where the Barlows live.
Wayne Barlow is twenty-two years old,
and sleeps in the backyard shed.
He has slick-black hair
with a duck's ass cut.
He wears tight hipsters,
wrinkle-sole shoes,
and rides a motorbike like a threat.
Keith and me hide in the bushes
waiting for Wayne
to thunder home from the pub
with a girl holding tight behind.
They stumble into
Wayne's lair.
I learn the weight of a breast,
the curve of a hip,
the weird rhythms and sounds
naked bodies make.

Keith and me,

numb from the eyes down,

watch

the folds of flesh

quiver and bend,

grateful

the Barlows are too poor

to afford curtains.

LOVE AND SEX: PART 1

At fourteen
I fall in love with Jane Russell,
Queen of Hollywood,
and Miss Spencer,
the secretary at school.
Eve Spencer is
eighteen years old,
with flawless skin,
a ponytail,
and breasts
that keep me awake long nights.
I start looking at girls
in my class with the same
cool half-closed eyes
that Wayne Barlow masters
looking at himself in the mirror
as he works on his hairstyle
late Friday
while the girl gets dressed.
Keith and me,
still in the bushes,
aren't sure
whether to look at her bra,
or at Wayne Barlow,
in love with himself
in the mirror.

LOVE AND SEX: PART 2

Miss Spencer lives
five doors down from me.
I wait for her in the fig tree
near the school gate.
She says,
"Hello, Harry. Walking home?"
I jump down and
offer to take her bag.
She asks after Dad,
and Keith,
and whether
my schoolwork is going well.
I say "fine"
to each question,
unable to take my eyes
off the bounce of her ponytail
as we walk home.
Miss Spencer and me.

DARLING, I LOVE YOU

Sometimes before school,
Keith and me crawl
under the train station waiting room
and inch our way
to the platform.
Through a gap in the floorboards
we watch well-dressed couples
holding hands, talking,
waiting for the Express
to the city.
We choose the
best-dressed pair
and crawl, face-up,
until we're under
their polished leather shoes.
We wait until
the woman looks away,
expecting the train,
then I say,
in my deepest voice,
"Darling, I love you."
She turns,
squeezes the man's hand,
smiles,
and says,

"Darling, I love you too."
Keith and me
bite down on our hands
to stop ourselves
from exploding with laughter.
We scramble out,
dust ourselves off,
as Keith throws his arms wide,
"Darling, I love you,"
dancing
behind the train station waiting room.

SATURDAY AFTERNOON

Miss Spencer
sits on the front step
in the sunshine
reading a book.
I call Keith
and ask him
for a game of soccer—
something I'm good at.
I score goal after goal,
dancing and cheering
each brilliant move
past Keith,
one eye on the ball,
one eye on Miss Spencer,
who looks up
and smiles
as I work even harder
to beat my brother,
who would rather be
riding his bike,
or flying his whirligig,
anything
but watching his big brother
make a fool of himself,
in the middle of Keeling Street,
on Saturday afternoon.

ROASTING

It's my turn to mow
the grass and weeds
we call a backyard.
I mow from front to back,
like Dad has shown me.
I can feel the
dull vibrations of the two-stroke
as I look for rocks.
I watch, keen
ever since Keith
hit a rock a year ago
and it flew out
and killed a hen.
Dad was so mad
he made Keith
pluck the dead bird.
Dad gutted it.
I coated it in oil
and put it in the oven.
It was the best chicken
we'd ever eaten.
Later, Keith told me
it was worth the roasting
he copped from Dad—
the taste of a fresh-dead
chicken.

LOVE AND SEX: PART 3

I switch the fuel to "off"
and wait for the mower to stop.
Then I walk it down to the Spencers'.
I knock on the door.
Her mother opens it,
still in a nightgown
even though it's late afternoon.
I offer to mow her lawn.
She says,
"Do what you want, kid,"
and slams the door shut.
It takes me an hour,
and when I'm finished,
Miss Spencer
comes out
and sits with me,
says thanks,
and hands me a drink.
I know I'll dream tonight
of her wearing that black top
with the hipster tights,
and that smile
spreading through my sleep.

ALL THE TIME

They aren't mad,
just slow.
The Hart twins.
Boys of fifteen
with pants pulled up high,
shiny black shoes,
thick-rimmed glasses
and hair pressed neat,
smelling of Brylcreem.
The gossips at Evans'
say it runs in the family—
like freckles
and crooked teeth.
Look at the husband.
No one waters a lawn
five hours a day, every day,
no one with a mind.
And Mrs. Hart,
buying dog food
months after the dog died,
and always saying,
"My, my, look at the sky crying,"
every time it rains.
Ashley Hart shares his
bag of lollies with Keith

every day.

And William Hart

grins constantly,

even during math,

and always puts his hand up first.

In all the years I've known him,

he's never once

given the correct answer,

grinning,

all the time.

LOVE AND SEX (AND PAIN)

Keith and me
in the bushes
each sucking on a caramel toffee,
waiting.
The thunder of Wayne's motorbike
shakes the ground
as we hide,
eyes wide.
They both wear
leather jackets
and helmets,
as they embrace
and slip into the shed.
Keith and me swallow hard,
our toffee forgotten
as Wayne's hand
moves under her top,
her hair long and silk shiny,
their bodies press together,
then,
in the dim light
I see her face.
"*NO!*"
I shout again, "*NO!*"
I pick up a rock,

hurl it blind,
turn and run,
Keith fast behind
as the glass shatters
and doors bang.
I don't stop
until bedroom safe.
I cover my face
with the pillow
and see
Miss Spencer
with Wayne's hand
creeping around,
and I cry
and swear
and spend all night
thinking
about Miss Spencer
and hating Wayne Barlow
forever.

A MATTER OF TIME

Johnny Barlow
stands in a circle of kids.
"My brother said
if he finds out who done it,
more than a window will get broken.
And he gave me this pound note, see,
if anyone knows,
well,
the money is theirs, okay?"
Johnny waves the tempting note
under our noses
and looks in our eyes.
"My brother says
it's only a matter of time
until he finds out.
Only a matter of time."
I look across at Keith.
His hands are
deep in his pockets,
but, even so,
I know they're shaking,
as Johnny
walks the circle,
waving the blood money
under each eager nose.
Only a matter of time.

GOOD LUCK

After dinner
my dad sits with his book
while Keith washes the dishes,
and I stare at the jigsaw puzzle
that is my homework.
Dad closes the book,
pushes his chair back,
and says,
"Wayne Barlow was
at the pub today."
I see Keith's shoulders tense
as I try hard
to study the puzzle.
"He was telling everyone
about some boys
who broke his shed window."
The puzzle blurs
before my eyes.
"He said Johnny
will find them.
He said a pound
was worth the price."
Keith turns to Dad,
his hands wet
with soapy water,

and I say, quickly,
"Yeah, Dad.
We heard Johnny today,
promising . . . "
My voice catches
as Dad opens the book,
and says,
"I drank my beer,
and wished Wayne
good luck."

BETTER THAN CATFISH

We get fishing line
from Evans' Grocery,
and wind it around an
empty Coke bottle.
A box of hooks
and sinkers cost a shilling.
Bait is easy—
worms dug from the scrapheap.
Keith and me
ride our bikes
across town to the big river
and sit in the shade
under the bridge
with cars speeding by
overhead.
I grip the head of the bottle
and fling the line,
watching it unravel
and splash in the current.
All we ever catch
are catfish.
They jump and squirm,
as we remove the hook.
Keith holds the fish close
and barks,

and meows,

before tossing it back.

It's rumored that

only the Hart boys

take the fish home

for catfish stew

with lots of salt

and spices

to hide the taste of mud.

Most of the time

Keith and me

catch snags,

or weeds,

or an old boot.

Keith grabs the boot,

and suggests we take it home.

For cooking?

"Better than catfish!"

LOVE AND SEX (AND MORE PAIN)

They say

she's left her job

at school

because she's "up the duff,"

and everyone reckons it's

Wayne Barlow,

who

wears leathers,

and a duck's ass,

and tight black jeans,

but never,

never

wears a frenchie.

I stand opposite

the Spencer house,

curtains drawn,

smoke rising from the wood stove,

and a dull ache

works its way

across my stomach.

Miss Spencer

comes downstairs

with a suitcase,

and a scarf

around her hair,

like the women
wore to Mum's funeral.
She looks up
and sadly smiles at me
as she slips into the taxi—
the first taxi I've ever seen
in Keeling Street—
taking away
the only good thing
left in town.
I pick up a rock,
fist-size,
and walk to the Barlow house.

CHOICE

Late at night,
safe in bed,
my hands still shaking,
my ears ringing
with the sound of breaking glass
and shouted threats,
I smirk
at the thought
of what I've done.

The Barlow family—
one old drunk,
one bikie,
one jailbird,
and one with the
quickest fists in school—
and Harry "Houdini" Hodby
throwing rocks,
not words.

Get out of this one, Harry!

A WEEK'S WAGE

The news
sweeps the playground
like a summer whirlwind.
Wayne Barlow
has been rocked again
and this time
he's offered five pounds.
Five pounds!
A week's wage in the foundry
for any information.
Urger and Fats
reckon
it's a gang
from another town
out to get Wayne,
or some enemies
of Mick Barlow
still locked
in Millthorpe Prison.
Johnny challenges every kid
in the school.
Cries of "It wasn't me"
follow in his wake.
I know the time will come.
Johnny will get me

on the oval,

or near the toilets;

he'll grab my shirt,

clench his fist,

and threaten

to shake the truth out.

But I know

Miss Spencer

deserves more

than having to leave town

in shame.

More than words

flung around Evans' Grocery

by people

with too much time

and too little brains.

So Johnny,

and his brother's money,

are powerless

against my hate.

TOO MUCH MONEY

Dad cuts the watermelon
in thick slices
and hands them
to Keith and me.
"Five pounds," he says.
"A lot of money.
Too much money
for a broken window."
Keith wants to tell.
I can see it in his eyes.
Dad looks at me
for a long time,
not saying a word,
then he reaches
for the knife
to cut another slice.
He says,
"Wayne must have done something,
for anybody to risk payback
from the Barlows.
Don't you reckon, Harry?"
I wipe the juice
from my mouth
and say,
"I'm sure he did, Dad."

Dad nods at my answer
as he throws the rind
onto the scrapheap,
and wipes the knife
on the tea towel
tucked into his shirt.

DURRA CREEK

I stay close to the banks
of the creek.
I climb over
the honeysuckle vine
as I walk upstream.
I hear the magpies
calling from the paperbarks.
I keep walking
for hours
until I reach
the open paddocks
flowering with grevillea
and gooseberries.
It's here the spring
bubbles out
from the rocks.
I spend the afternoon
lying in the wild grass
looking up at the immense sky
listening
to the steady murmur
of Durra Creek
being born.

CRICKET

My dad always says,
"People play cricket
with their souls,
as well as their hands."
I don't know
what he means
until I see Johnny Barlow
running in to bowl
and the ball bounces clear
over Urger's head.
He turns to Johnny
and says,
"Bet you can't do it again."
Johnny doesn't.
He bowls a full toss
that hits Urger
on the shoulder
and rolls
down to the boundary
for four.
After they bandage
Urger's shoulder,
and help him off the field,
I come in to bat.
Johnny bowls

an over

at full pace.

I watch each ball

go by

missing the stumps

by a whisker.

At the end of the over

Johnny walks up and says,

"Too scared to hit them, Hodby?"

When Johnny bowls again

I do the same.

I watch,

and I wait

HOUDINI?

The next day
Johnny meets me
on the way home.
He blocks my path
and says,
"I've asked everyone, Hodby.
Except you,
and Keith."
He lets the sentence hang.
I stand my ground.
Johnny says,
"No one at school
is smart enough to lie, Hodby.
Except you."

I can feel the sweat
under my shirt
and a cold shiver
tingles up my spine.
I know Johnny
is waiting for me
to deny it,
or blame someone else.
Then he'll see it,
in my eyes.

The lie.

I put my hands

deep in my pockets

and shrug,

"Why would Keith and me

bother with your brother, Johnny?"

He tries to think of an answer

and I follow with a quick,

"If we're going to stone anyone's house,

it'd be bloody Peter Evans,

for sure.

Don't you reckon?"

It sounds true,

and in Johnny's mind,

it is true.

We all hate Peter.

I step around Johnny,

"See you tomorrow."

Johnny hesitates,

and I walk away.

PAYBACK

It's been a week
since Wayne got rocked
and the schoolyard agrees
it was payback
from a gang
Wayne must have crossed.
Johnny's stopped talking about it.
Only Urger keeps asking,
annoyed he can't find the culprit,
thinking of what he could do
with five pounds.
He's even taken to asking
the young kids in Primary,
scaring them so much
one little boy
ran to the teacher.
We all laughed at Urger,
on detention
for a week,
still penniless.
I joked,
"Hey, Urger,
pick on someone your own size,
next time!"

PEARCE SWAMP

I take off my clothes
and place them,
folded,
on a rock.
I walk slowly into
the cold water
and swim to the middle.
A mild ripple
creases the surface
as I roll
on my back
and look up
through the red gums
to the cloudless sky.
My breath is slow in my ears.
It's all I hear
as I float,
knowing
I'm alone
with the ghost
of the swamp,
somewhere
near the weeping willows.
No one visits this place,
except me

and the mysterious ring-bearer.
At school
Linda
would sit near the oval,
surrounded by girls.
They talked
of music,
and clothes,
and the secrets of the weekend,
until the rainstorm
drove them all indoors,
except Linda,
holding out her hands
to catch the heavy drops
that ran down her cheeks
like perfect tears.

FOUR   MY FATHER'S HANDS

A DAY EARLY

It's Tuesday
and Aunt Alice arrives
without lamingtons,
without the white tablecloth,
and she doesn't even bother
to check for dirt
behind our ears.
Me and Keith are worried.
We sit at the kitchen table
and together say, "Where's Dad?"
Aunt Alice takes off her lopsided hat,
smoothes her dress,
which never has a crease,
and boils some water.
"You boys like tea, don't you?"
Now we are scared.
Every Wednesday
we have tea and lamingtons
made by Aunt Alice
and here she is,
a day early
with the look of a rabbit
caught in the spotlight.
I leap up
and shout,

"Where's Dad?"
as the kettle boils
in our big empty kitchen.

A LUCKY MAN

The lathe
came down on his finger
like a guillotine.
It severed the bone,
the tendons,
and spat it across the factory floor,
where Henry Johns
picked it up
and put it in a bag full of ice.
My dad pushed the red button
with his good hand
and called to Henry
before he fell to one knee,
wrapping a rag
around where his finger should be.
The doctors spent two hours
trying to sew it back,
while Dad,
wide-eyed and numb,
looked at the damage.
By late afternoon they gave up.
They sewed the finger closed
and told Dad he was a lucky man.
Dad started dressing,
despite the protests of the nurses.

He covered the sling
with his overcoat
as he walked out,
"a lucky man"
riding the train home,
one finger less.

WHISPER

Aunt Alice stays late,
washes the dishes,
tells me I'm a good cook,
and wipes the kitchen clean.
Keith and me sit in bed,
waiting for Dad.
He comes in
and kisses us both.
The first kiss
since the night after Mum died.
He closes the door
and walks down the hallway
to the kitchen
and Aunt Alice's tears.
Keith rolls over
and whispers to me
in the dark,
"Harry, don't sleep on your left side.
That's where your heart is.
Don't sleep on your heart."

MAYBE, JOHNNY

The next day
Johnny Barlow asks me about Dad.
I shrug,
not sure what Dad would want me to say.
"He's okay.
He'll be back at work in a few days."
Johnny and me stand,
hands in our pockets,
watching
the young kids play marbles.
Johnny says,
"People who die don't leave.
If you listen at night,
you can hear their voices."
I look up at the sun through the pines.
I've never heard anyone
talk like this.
I don't hear my mum's voice.
All I hear at night
is Keith snoring,
or the slap of the wind
on our timber shutters.
I look at Johnny
and say,
"Maybe, Johnny."

We keep watching the marbles,
our thoughts
on the dark
and the voices.

VOICES

Mick Barlow
received two years jail,
no parole,
for beating up
a businessman
in the city
and stealing his wallet
and fancy watch.
Mick Barlow
should have sold the watch,
not worn it
for all the world
and the cops
to see.
And Old Man Barlow
lines up
empty beer bottles
on his back fence
and takes potshots
with his .22
until he's too drunk
to hold the rifle steady.
And Wayne.
I hate Wayne.
Motorbikes,

the pub,

and girls.

Mrs. Barlow spends her days

on the verandah,

knitting,

and screaming at Wayne

to stop revving his ugly bike.

The Barlows live

at the dead end

of Dylan Street.

And Johnny?

How can he hear voices

with all that noise?

MY DAD'S GOOD HAND

The three of us in the backyard,
a watermelon between.
My dad, with his arm
still in a sling,
gives me the knife
and shows me how to cut,
holding the melon
with his left hand.
I grip the knife
with all my force
in case it slips and cuts Dad,
his fingers inches from the blade,
pressing into the rind.
I see the spider veins on his hand,
leading up to the watch
with the leather band
he wears, even in bed.
Dad only uses sharp knives.
I cut easily,
and we eat
two slices each,
and I know
that my job from now on,
as well as cooking,
is cutting the watermelon.

I look at Keith,
proud
that I can be trusted
with Dad's good hand.

ONE SUNDAY AT A TIME

I know
because
he's quieter than usual
on Sunday,
and he sweeps Mum's gravestone
slowly,
and I see him
touch his lips
with his good hand
and run it gently
over Mum's name.
He gives us money
for chips.
Keith runs to the shop.
I hide behind
the tiered headstone
of some long-dead
rich man,
out of Dad's view,
and I watch.
In the stillness
I see his lips moving,
telling Mum
about the adventures
of our days.

Their wedding anniversary.
The merciless sun
heating the cool stone
where I sit
watching my dad—
his gentle hands
tracing this special day
through his other life,
through his memory.

SO STUPID

Sometimes
when Dad is late home,
Keith and me ride
across town
to the Pines Golf Club.
We walk
the green fairways
with a hessian bag,
searching for balls
lost by golfers too rich
to look
in the long grass,
or under poplars
the size of skyscrapers.
We run to the 15th
and slide into the dam,
water knee-high,
feeling for golf balls
with our feet
in the dark sand.
We throw them
on the bank to dry.
At dusk
we gather our bag
and return to the clubhouse

where
Mr. Newberry
gives us a pound
for a bag of balls.
Keith and me listen
to Mr. Newberry talk about golf.
"A good walk spoiled,"
he says.
We nod
and wonder at how
rich people get rich
when they are so stupid,
and so lazy.

SELLING OR BUYING

Old Mrs. Spencer sits
on the fold-up chair
on the verandah
holding a metal tin
as neighbor after neighbor
walks through the house,
touching china,
kitchen scales,
bakelite canisters,
a cardigan with a leather patch,
a faded quilt,
and gathers what they need,
or can afford,
and drops the money
into Mrs. Spencer's tin.
The coins echo
like a slap across the face.
I run home,
reach under the wardrobe
for the five shillings
I've been saving for a football.
In Miss Spencer's room
is a silver locket
on a chain.
I drop the coins

into the tin.
Mrs. Spencer burps,
and swears,
and closes her eyes
to the sun.

WORK

Each morning
I hear the pigeons first.
The pecking against the cool iron.
I see a light
from Dad's room,
and I know
he's buttoning
the blue flannelette shirt
and pulling on his gray overalls.
He goes into the bathroom
and splashes cold water
on his face and hair.
He takes the tortoiseshell comb
and makes a crooked part
on the left side.
In the kitchen
he lights the stove
for porridge,
sits reading the paper
and the news
of an earthquake in Turkey.
At 6:30
he closes the back door,
lifts the bike down
from the hook

under the stairs
and rides through
the frosty streets,
humming a tune
he learned in church
when he was eight years old
and hadn't begun
to think of
work,
or loneliness,
or pain,
or growing old
one factory day
at a time.

DIRECTIONS OUT

My dad once said,

"You go left at the grocery.

Follow that road for a mile,

sharp right where the sawmill

sends the dust high.

Then left, after the river.

That leads you through the Kelly farm.

Those cows, dairy mainly,

and a few prize bulls

living the life . . .

Okay, take a left at the T-junction.

You go along that road,

new bitumen,

no potholes for a few years,

even gutters for the storm water,

until you see the dry-stone wall

on the right,

built years ago,

and still standing.

Turn right,

follow that for a few miles

until you reach the major intersection,

then . . .

well, you can turn left or right,

it doesn't matter,

because, by then
you're miles
and another world away
from here."

EMPTY SKY

I remember
climbing the oak tree
near the railway tracks
and watching them load
Linda's coffin onto the train.
I watched Mr. Mahony
lift his eyes from the casket
and look into the empty sky.
He stood, head raised,
with both hands
clenching his heart
as if to stop it beating,
staring
into the infinite blue.
I sat in the oak
and watched the Mahony family,
and my friend Linda,
leave town.

FIVE   STORM SEASON

STORM SEASON

The storm rises over Rookwood Hill
all purple and dark blue,
and the lightning
snaps electricity
as everyone reaches
for matches and kerosene lamps.
Dad slams our shutters tight
and locks the hens
in the shed.
Keith and me lift our bikes
onto the hooks under the stairs,
remembering last year's flood
that swept them down Keeling Street
to be found later,
muddy and foul,
two streets away.
The thunder shakes
the kitchen floor
while I watch
raindrops pound the chook shed
and pockmark the ground.
It rains like this
for three days
as gutters overflow
and yards become pools,

streets become rivers,

until Pearce Swamp

rises higher than the train line

and the water smells

of rotten fruit,

sugarcane,

and thick mud.

Everyone watches the banks

of the big river

with nervous eyes,

remembering.

Then it stops.

The flood disappears overnight

as if someone has pulled a plug

at Hobsons Bend

and let it all slip away

as we sleep.

HARD AND CRACKED

The next day
I go to Linda's cross.
The ring and the daisies
are gone.
I wander around
amongst the flattened weeds,
ragged willows,
and the stinking mud.
I find dead fish,
empty bottles,
and somebody's lawn mower.

I sit on a log and cry,
as the mud under my feet
dries hard and cracked,
in the midday sun.

DREAMS

At night
I dream of my mother
standing beside Pearce Swamp,
waving from across the water.
Calling me,
to dive in?
I swim across the
cool clear water
and scramble out.
I see Linda's cross,
nothing else.
I look back
and watch Mum
disappear into the bushes.
I sit by Linda's cross,
dripping wet,
listening to the
pressing silence.

MISSING

Johnny Barlow disappears
the night the flood recedes.
They search the forest
with tracker dogs
but only find Birdy,
high in a rivergum,
still on guard.
They dive in Pearce Swamp.
Old Man Barlow
puts up posters
in nearby towns
and swears off the drink.
Wayne cruises the outskirts
of town on his bike,
scaring the cows
and smoking endless cigarettes
on Rookwood Hill.
The town is quiet,
sure that bad luck
has come again.

THE PRICE OF SYMPATHY

Mr. Evans says,
"Johnny's run away,
but he'll be back.
And if he was my kid,
I'd know where to look,
but anyway,
if he was my son
he wouldn't run away
in the first place.
That's the trouble
with young kids today.
No discipline.
No honesty.
Didn't he break my Peter's racket?
He'll be back.
He'll turn out like his brother,
locked in jail.
Good for nothing.
One problem less in town.
That's one way of looking at it.
Don't you agree, Mr. Hodby?"

Dad packs the groceries
into his work bag
and looks at Mr. Evans

for a long time,

then answers,

"No. I don't agree,

Mr. Evans."

Dad and I walk out

and I can breathe again.

JUST LIKE JOHNNY

I know Johnny is safe.
How?
Because I remember
the gossip last year
about Linda
and how people said
she tried to surf the flood.
They gabbed about it for days.
And now, the ladies
at Evans' Grocery
go on and on
about this town
and its bad luck,
its curse.
On and on about
the floods
that come in the night
and suck the life
out of this place.
I know it won't be long
before they start on
about Miss Spencer,
or Mr. Kerry,
or Mum.
I know Johnny is safe

because after listening
to all these ugly little voices
I want to run away, too.
Just like Johnny.

THE THREAT

After three days
Old Man Barlow
lets it be known
that food is missing
from his fridge,
and Johnny has been seen
outside the town
near the forest.
"He isn't home yet,
but when he is,
he'll get an earful."
We all know
what that means,
and as I trudge to school,
with the galahs
cackling in the trees
and the heat shimmer
rising from the road,
I hope Johnny
has enough food
to last forever,
deep in the forest
where his dad can't reach,
and where he can't see
the knowing smirk

on Mr. Evans' face
every time
a customer walks in.

THE RHYTHM OF THE FOREST

I pack my schoolbag
with cheese and vegemite sandwiches,
two water bottles,
and a bag of apples.
I shoulder the load
and walk through
the still Sunday
to where the road turns
away from the forest.
I climb the fence
and follow the track,
overgrown
with bottlebrush and myrtle.
I walk for an hour
to where the shadows,
cool and dark,
spread long fingers
over every step.
All I can hear are frogs,
rhythmic and low,
and my heart,
beating,
waiting for Johnny
to appear.

JOHNNY'S PLACE

Johnny sits on a log
and eats the sandwiches,
shines the apple
on his dirty pants
before taking a grateful bite,
and laughs at the idea
of his dad putting up posters.
"So what did it say?
'If anyone sees this
little bastard,
send him home
or clip him behind the ear
once for me.'"
Johnny tosses the core
into the undergrowth
and looks at me,
deciding if I can be trusted,
or not.
"When the flood came,
I had to leave.
I couldn't sit in my room,
just watching the rain."
I think I understand.
I say,
"Every time a storm blows,

people close their doors,

and hope it goes away.

As if turning their backs

will stop it, or something . . . "

Johnny answers,

"Nothing can stop it, Hodby.

Nothing."

We're both quiet,

thinking of last year's flood,

and the damage it caused.

"You liked Linda,

didn't you, Hodby?"

I'm surprised by the question.

I say I did.

I say she was my friend.

I say she was the only girl

I talked to in our class.

I say she was too good for this town.

Then I stop talking

because I see Johnny

staring into the forest,

and I sense that here—

deep in the bush

where no one from town ventures,

where Birdy keeps watch for invaders,

where catfish and eels

swim in the creeks,
where creepers and giant ferns grow—
here, by my answer
I've wandered,
without thinking,
into Johnny's place.

PUNISHMENT

Johnny says,
"Do you remember, Hodby?
Last year,
during prayers,
when Linda got caught
talking,
and smiling?
'Smiling at Jesus,' the priest said,
as if that was a crime?
Remember he ordered Linda
to sit with the boys,
as punishment?
And all the girls giggled.
And nose-picking Craig Randall,
Urger,
and everyone else
spread out on the chairs
to stop Linda sitting.
Remember?
And Linda walked
straight up the back,
where you and me were,
and sat beside us.
I saw you smile, Hodby,
pleased she chose you.
Well, Harry,
she sat between us, remember?"

ALONE

On the way home,
I stop at Pearce Swamp.
I sit by the water
and stare
at the hanging willows.
The tips of their branches
touch the water,
sending ripples across
with each gust of wind.

Tell me, Linda?
What happened here?
Were you swimming?
Or surfing the flood,
like they say?
Or just trying to cross the creek,
walking, arms spread,
balancing on a moss-covered log,
and you slipped?

I think you were lying here,
on the grassy bank,
staring at the rain-filled sky,
unaware of the torrent,
writing another story,

smiling at the thought
of reading it to the class.
Tell me, Linda?
Were you alone?

DUST

Johnny comes home
the next day
as a dust storm
blows in from the drylands
out west,
where rain never falls,
covering everything
in a dirty pall
that you can taste
on your lips
and feel on your skin.
People dip hankies in water
and cover their mouths.
Evans' closes.
The school sends us all home.
And Johnny
walks slowly
down Musgrave Road
in four-day dirty clothes,
grateful
the town has something
to talk about other than
the Barlow boy returning
and what his old man will do
when he sees him
walk through the door.

DEAL

The schoolyard
hasn't been this quiet in a while.
Johnny Barlow is sitting
under the pine trees
doing nothing but stare
at the school and everyone
through his two black eyes,
swollen, half-closed.
Fats and Red bet
it was his dad,
a pound each,
against Scuzz,
who's sure it was Wayne.
But how to find out?
Urger says I should ask.
Or we should get a girl to ask.
He wouldn't hit a girl, would he?
By lunchtime Urger has collected
sixty shillings on bets,
but still
no one has an answer.
I take the pound note
Keith and I earned
collecting golf balls,
place it into Urger's greedy hands,

and say,

"My money's on Mrs. Barlow."

Everyone laughs and calls me stupid.

I walk over and sit beside Johnny.

He turns and asks,

"How much is in the pot?"

"Sixty shillings, and my pound,

and I've been sent to find out who."

Johnny rubs his swollen eyes,

smiles, and says,

"Sixty/forty split, okay?

For whoever you said."

I suggest, "Fifty/fifty?"

Johnny punches my arm,

and says,

"I've got the black eyes.

It's sixty/forty. Deal?"

"Deal."

SIX SOMEONE, SOMETIME

SOMEONE, SOMETIME

In summer,
around midday,
on a Saturday
when the tired afternoon haze
draws everyone,
even the flies,
to sleep in the shade,
I walk
to the house on Longden Street.
The corner house.
A two-story weatherboard,
painted clean white,
with every window closed,
shutting out
the lazy breeze
blowing across the railway tracks.
I stand opposite
and stare
at the lawn,
green and flat like carpet,
cut to perfection.
The concrete path
painted rust red,
like long-dried blood.
I stand alone

in the stupefying heat,

marvelling

at the house

with no trees

no shrubs

no flowers

no garden ornaments,

nothing

but the funeral lawn

and closed windows.

Someone

must live there.

Someone must

mow that grass

in the shadeless heat.

Someone,

sometime.

LOVE AND SEX AND BROTHERS

My brother Keith
and Sally Anderson
are hiding
in the bush cubby
we built years ago
near the Army Reserve.
I sit against the gum tree
with my pocketknife.
I carve my name
and listen.
All I hear
is the wind,
a crow in the tree above,
and Sally's giggles.
I kid myself
I'm looking out for Keith,
making sure he's left alone
with his girl.
But I'm thinking
of Miss Spencer
getting bigger
and rounder
and spending her afternoons
waiting,
feeling the world

sneer behind her back.
I carve her name
into the lonely gum
and wonder
if anyone in this small town
will see it
and care to remember.

BEFORE YOU SLEEP

Newspapers
and books.
Every morning
Dad reads the *Sun*
over breakfast.
He shakes his head,
sips his tea,
and turns each page
with silent anger.
But at night
he sits
in his big old chair
and reads novels
about a girl
running across the Moors
in the middle of England,
and the travels
of a man
deep into the jungle,
looking for gold.
Sometimes
I watch Dad read.
An hour passes
before he knows I'm there.
So far away

on a farm,

in a jungle,

on a ship rocked by waves.

When he looks up

from the pages

and sees me,

I grin and say,

"You're back."

He laughs

as he places his bookmark

between the pages.

He hands me the book,

and says,

 "It's a nice place to visit, Harry.

You know that?

A nice place to visit,

before you sleep."

LOVE

I wake
to Keith's snoring
and I swear he whispered
"Sally" in his dream.
Love?
I tiptoe to the kitchen,
open the creaking door
and sit on the back step,
listening to the town.
The moon
is a shiny silver fingernail
that throws enough light
for me to see the cane toads
hopping silently around the yard.
A rooster crows
from across the railway tracks
and I check my watch.
Fifteen minutes
until Dad wakes.
I return to the kitchen,
take the old metal saucepan,
and empty two cups of porridge,
some water and milk,
and place it quietly
on the stove.

Today
is Dad's birthday.
And no matter
how young or old you are,
you shouldn't make breakfast—
not on your birthday.
Not in the cool dark.
Not on a Monday.
Not alone.
Not without someone you love,
and someone who loves you.

AFTERNOON SOCCER

Scuzz takes the penalty
and misses
because,
as he kicks,
Red and Grease
yell,
"Scuzz can't hit a barn door."
And he can't,
but he chases those two
until he corners them.
Grease, true to his name,
slips through the fence,
but Red
is sorry,
and even sorrier to be caught,
as Urger urges the fight.
And Scuzz proves
he can hit a barn door,
and Red,
beaten black and red,
blames Grease,
who slips out of sight
and doesn't come to school
for the rest of the week
while

Scuzz practices his shot
every afternoon
without saying a word.

FOLLOW THE BATS

"You follow the bats."
That's how you find
the ripe mangoes.
At dusk,
watch the bats
circling over the fig trees
near Cowpers Paddock.
The noise is ear-splitting,
as they squabble and chatter,
covering the trees
like hanging black fruit.
After sunset,
they wheel across the sky
to the river
and the trees
near Hobsons Bend.
If you're lucky,
and you've got the stamina
to fight through the dandelions
and jimson weed,
and you've got earplugs
for all that noise,
you might find a ripe mango
but
you'd better be quick.

CATCH

I see Keith walking down the street
tossing a tennis ball in the air,
catching it every few steps,
whistling.
I know he's been to the old cubby
with Sally,
exploring . . .
I walk outside,
wait on our footpath,
as Keith motions for me
to catch the ball
he'll toss the fifty yards
between us.
It sails high.
He's thrown too hard.
I skip back fast
and fall
as the ball drops
into my outstretched hand.
Keith whistles and applauds.
I stand,
dust myself off,
and wait for my brother
to reach the gate
before I hand him the ball.

I can run.

I can dive.

I can catch,

and yes, I can throw,

but

the last time I threw,

I threw rocks.

HATE

Plovers!
Dive-bombing!
We run around the oval,
our feet prickled by bindi-eyes.
The teachers wave us inside
while we pretend
not to notice,
chasing the ball
with one hand held high—
the plover salute.
Nothing but lightning
stops our lunchtime game,
until
Peter Evans
finds two baby birds
chirping for food
and safety.
He takes them
upstairs to the verandah,
holds them, featherless,
in his big useless hands,
and throws them
high into the air.
They splatter
onto the concrete below.

Peter grins wildly,

chanting,

"Birds can't fly,

birds can't fly."

Keith and me stand on the oval

and decide

we hate plovers,

lightning,

bindi-eyes,

and teachers calling us inside,

but

most of all,

we hate Peter.

MONEY FOR SONG

Peter's family
drives a brand-new
midnight blue Holden,
with venetian blinds
across the back window,
and a little toy dog
nodding on the dashboard.
They drive to church
on Sunday evening,
and sit in the front row,
Peter smiling between
his parents.
Mr. Evans
passes the plate,
making sure
everyone sees him
put a pound note in first.
And with a satisfied smirk
he hands it to Mrs. Barlow,
here alone, as usual,
who drops in a coin
and passes it on, quickly.
I watch all this
from upstairs,
where I hide,

where no one ever sits,

where I can hear

the sweet strong voices

of the choir

rising above

the sinners down below,

filling the church

with angels.

A NEW GIRL

A new girl
arrives in class today.
Claire.
Claire Honey.
You should hear
Urger,
snickering,
eager to show off his
dazzling humor
with pathetic jokes about,
"Honey, you're sweet."
"Crumpet and honey. Nice."
I decide to avoid
the usual places
this lunchtime.

Maybe I'll even
say hello to Claire.
Show her we're not
all like Urger,
or Scuzz,
leering from the back row,
or Craig Randall,
with one finger
still searching for a brain
through his nasal passage.

SMALL TOWN?

I walk up to Claire
at lunch,
and say,
"Welcome to school."
I mumble something
about our small town,
and how her family
at least makes it slightly bigger.

She punches my arm,
just lightly,
"Small?
This town's twice as big
as where we come from.
And it's got water—
a river, some creeks . . .
You can swim in summer, right?"
I nod,
surprised anyone
would look at my town like that.
I say,
"Yeah.
And we can fish, too.
Only catfish . . .
and yabbies."

Claire sits beside me
on the school fence,
and says,
"Well, if the catfish don't mind,
I'll swim all weekend."

FIREWORKS

"Like a classroom of boys
farting,
one after another."
That's what Dad says.
Tom Thumbs
are my favorite.
I light the wick,
wait until it burns down,
then throw it high.
Dogs howl while
me and Keith
roll on the grass in the park,
laughing.
Cheap.
Cheap and noisy.
Penny Bungers
are more serious.
We put them into drink cans
or cardboard boxes
and watch the sides blow—
the can dancing on the fencepost,
the box catching fire.
Star Wheels
are for girls.
I don't want colors,

or movement.

I want noise.

And noise

is the Tuppeny Bunger,

stuck in the Evans'

letterbox

at midnight.

We watch it kick high

into the air

before rattling and banging

onto the footpath.

Mr. Evans comes to the door

with a torch and a cricket bat.

Me and Keith,

already two streets away,

listening

to the dogs

go crazy.

OUR FATHER'S MOOD

Sometimes, after work,

he stands quiet

in the backyard,

hands on hips,

eyes lost in the distance

while Keith and me

clean the house,

cook the dinner,

and finish every piece of homework.

Stuff that doesn't need doing

gets done.

Our dad shuffles,

one foot to the other,

puts his hands in his pockets

and keeps staring

at the back fence

and the scrapheap.

Even the chickens keep away.

They peck at grass seed

and bob their stupid heads

without making a sound.

As night comes,

Dad turns and walks inside,

smiles at us boys,

the dinner ready,

the table set,

and we smile back,

sure our father's mood

has been left scattered over the yard

like grass seed,

eaten by quiet birds.

THE RAILWAY BRIDGES

It takes exactly
twenty-five seconds
to walk, double-time,
across the rail-bridges
over Durra Creek.
It's that,
or walk
half a mile downstream
to cross.
You choose one bridge,
clench your fists,
your teeth,
keep your eyes down
on each wooden sleeper
suspended
high over the swirling water,
and stride
across the inbound track,
listening for the train whistle
that warns you
twenty-five seconds,
twenty seconds,
to make the other side
or meet the freight train,
wailing.

Which track is it on?
Fifteen seconds,
ten seconds,
to take the dive
into Durra Creek,
water circling blindly
around granite boulders.
Which track is it on?
Five seconds, four, three.
Too late.
The train storms by
on the opposite bridge
as you sit and cry
and scream
at death
thundering away
on the outbound track.

THE OUTBOUND TRACK

I cross the bridge
and sit between the tracks
facing south,
listening to the creek
rush below.
The whistle
rattles back
as the train heads
towards the horizon.
Another storm is brewing
over Rookwood Hill.
I think of hiding
beside these tracks—
I'll wait for the next freight train
to rumble by,
and at the last minute,
I'll sprint and jump aboard.
No time to think,
or decide
where it's going.
Just jump.

The rain starts falling
in heavy drops
and a wind

comes down from the hill.

I walk across the blackberry paddock,

climb the old wire fence,

and turn into Musgrave Road,

ahead of the oncoming storm.

SOMETIME, SOMEDAY

Those that leave this town
don't come back.
Linda.
The Mahony family.
Mr. Kerry.
Miss Spencer.
I heard the talk
of a baby,
a girl,
interstate.
And those that stay
lock themselves tight,
or hide in the forest,
like Birdy,
forever waiting.
While the rest of us
tend crosses
and daisies
and sweep gravestones;
talk to ghosts,
and live quiet, steady lives
of half-memory.
I watch my dad
read books
with his faraway smile

and I try to understand.

I know,

someday,

sometime soon enough,

I'll have to choose.

And I know

my dad

has given me the directions out

in his strong, calm voice.

I remember them,

word for word.

I wait for that day.

I hear my father's voice.

CLAIRE'S RAIN

Claire stands under the awning
at Evans' Grocery,
eating an ice cream
and watching the rain fall.
She offers me a bite,
"Chocolate."
We sit and watch
the water rush down the street
and away to Durra Creek
at the bottom of the hill.
"I love the rain, Harry.
The smell, and the sound."
I look up at the heavy clouds
thinking of the damage
they've brought in the past.
Claire says,
"It cleans everything.
Fills the dams
and flushes the creeks.
It's like God starting again."
She finishes her ice cream,
puts on her raincoat
and starts to leave,
then turns and says,
"It's good to start again.
Don't you think, Harry?"

SEVEN **NOT ALONE**

FRIDAY EVENINGS

I remember
Friday evenings
in summer.
My mother,
in her purple dress
with the black belt,
would sit in the cane chair
on the verandah
with the music
soft and low,
waiting for my dad.
Keith and me
would read in the lounge
and I'd watch Mum
comb her black hair
until it shone.
She'd pour two glasses
of beer,
each with a full head,
when she saw Dad
turn the corner,
cruise down the hill
on his bicycle,
hands behind his back,
as Keith and me

jumped from the lounge,
"No hands, Dad,
No hands!"
He'd lean his body
into the driveway
and ride that bike
under the house,
never once touching
the handlebars,
while my mother
sat back in the chair
and pressed her hands
along the folds
of her soft purple dress,
ready for Friday evening
to dance
gently into view.

CLAIRE

Claire sits with me
sometimes.
She talks about
her old town:
a few streets of houses
with no fences,
a park with rusted swings,
a dry creek bed,
a wheat silo, disused,
and a cattle yard
on the road out,
where twice a year
they drive the trucks
up to the gates
and load the herds
who stamp and bellow
and send clouds of red dust
drifting over the town,
clinging to everything.
She looks at the kids
from Primary
chasing each other
through the pine grove
and says,
"You see those scrawny pines?
They'd call that a forest back home!"

TOO LATE

Mrs. Evans
from the grocery store
died
on Friday.
The principal
came to our class
for the first time ever
and asked Peter
to step outside.
We saw Peter's shoulders sag.
He didn't come back
for five days
and by then
we all knew
about
the dangers of smoking,
and no matter
how rich
or pretty
or smart
or funny
or religious
you are,
cancer
can get you,

and like the guard dogs
at Evans' Grocery,
it doesn't let go
until it's too late.

IT WASN'T GOD

It wasn't God
who screwed Miss Spencer
in the dark
late one Friday,
or
drove the taxi
slowly away, weeks later.
It wasn't God
who pressed the button
that sent the blade down
and tossed Dad's finger
onto the factory floor . . .
who drove the truck
skidding down into the river,
who watched the bubbles rising
and fists knocking
against a jammed window . . .
who put cancer
so deep into Mrs. Evans
that she coughed blood
all over the counter,
weighing potatoes for Dad . . .
who dragged Mum
quietly away,
with sadness in her eyes . . .

who sent the swirling water
down Pearce Swamp
where Linda . . .

It wasn't God.
It wasn't God.
He was away.
He was busy.
He was in some other town,
miles away.
It wasn't God.
Was it?

NOT ALONE

Today
at Pearce Swamp,
near the cross,
I see a dirt mound
with footprints
and a sweeping
spread over freshly turned ground.
I cross myself
and dig
with nervous hands.
The swamp is still
and quiet
as the earth
exposes
a tiny silver case
with a heart pattern
on the lid.

Inside
is another ring.

I close the lid gently,
polish the case with my shirt,
hold it for a long time.
Smiling to myself,

I bury the case,
the ring safely inside.
I cover my diggings,
and work
weeding the daisies
near Linda's cross,
pleased
I'm not alone
with Linda
in my memories.

A GIFT OF WAR

Wayne Barlow in uniform!
A soldier.
Our protector.
Our hero?
The duck's ass
cut to a stubble.
The leather jacket
hung carelessly
over a wooden chair
as he straightens his tie
and khaki jacket,
and salutes the mirror.
"Sir!"

Wayne Barlow with a gun!
His dad smiling
that twisted Barlow grin
as he slaps Wayne on the back
and says,
"Keep your head down, son."
The family pose
for photo after photo,
and in each one,
you can see Johnny
up the back

with his eyes firmly

focused

on Wayne's motorbike

in front of the shed.

A gift of war.

JOHNNY'S BIRTHDAY

He comes to school
in his brother's leather jacket
as if to say,
"My jacket, my bike."
He says Wayne
sent them a letter
from camp
hoping for a war soon,
and promising him the bike
until he got home.
The math teacher
clicks his fingers
for attention
and says,
"Happy birthday, Johnny.
As a special treat
we'll do a test first up,
shall we?"

COOKING

Linda's mum
loved to cook.
We'd all drop big hints
to Linda in class
that our birthday was soon.
Sometimes
we'd get lucky,
sometimes not.
I got a chocolate cake,
two-tiered,
with my age
written in cream.
Johnny got a box full
of rum balls
that we ate at lunchtime.
Six of us
sat in a circle
as Johnny
threw a rum ball
each our way.
I remember, now,
Linda was next to Johnny
and beamed
as he passed her
the last rum ball.

A PRESENT

I gather smooth rocks
and place them
in a small cardboard box.
I wrap the box
in red crepe paper,
and tie it with some string.
I carry the present
down to the swamp
and wait,
sure Johnny
will come here
to the cross
on his birthday.

OUR SWAMP

Johnny tears the wrapping, quickly.
I keep my eyes on him
as he reaches in
and pulls out
one of the rocks.
It's flat, smooth
and shiny black.
Johnny tosses it
from hand to hand,
not sure what to do,
what to say,
what it means.
I say,
"I've given the Barlows
a few of those before.
But never in broad daylight."
Johnny stares across the swamp,
still holding the rock,
his eyes set on the far bank
and the thick forest beyond.
He shakes his head,
and laughs,
"So it *was* you!
You're a good liar, Hodby.
Better than me."

I nod, and say,
"Because of Miss Spencer."
Johnny stands,
and with one sharp side-arm throw
skims the rock across
the surface of the water.
Then he picks up another
and hurls it as high as he can.
It splashes in the middle
of Pearce Swamp,
making a deep, satisfying sound.
Johnny passes a rock to me,
"Have a go, Harry."
We spend the rest of the afternoon
tossing rocks into the swamp.
Pearce Swamp.
Linda's swamp.
Our swamp.

LISTENING

Johnny hears a voice
late at night.
Linda whispers solace
in the bitterness of the Barlow house.
He polishes his boxing gloves
or he sits at his desk
looking out at Wayne's shed,
and the motorbike,
and his dad's empty bottles.
Linda whispers,
and Johnny hears
"because he can."

My dad listens
all night
in his old lounge chair
with a cup of tea.
He stares into space
and remembers her voice,
and the smell of her hair,
and her long hands
pressing the folds of her dress.
And if you'd ask him
to move on,
he'd look at you

with those clear beautiful eyes
and he'd smile
and touch your arm
and say, "To where?"
Then he'd go back
to his chair
and listen
to Keith snoring
in the next room,
or he'd check on me
quiet in bed.
He'd close our door,
return to his chair,
and listen
all night
to the miraculous sound
of her presence.

HOW LONG?

Claire sits beside
the big river,
dangling her feet
in its steady flow.
She picks up a branch
and throws it downstream.
"How long before
it reaches the ocean, Harry?
One week? Two weeks?"
I sit beside her,
squelch my toes
in the thick mud
and say,
"I don't know.
But wouldn't it be fun
to float that easily?"
Claire laughs,
stands, and dives
into the cool water,
swimming calmly
to the middle of the river.
She waves back at me
and calls,
"Come on, Harry.
It's wonderful."

I take off my shirt,
walk along the bank
to where the rope is tied
to the old rivergum.
I grab the rope tightly,
take a running jump,
and let go.

MY FATHER'S ROOM

Sometimes, when I'm home,
and it's hours until Dad returns,
and I know Keith is with Sally
near the Army Reserve,
I go into my father's room.
I sit on his bed
and look at the photos
on his dresser.
The one of Keith and me
sitting in the crook of a tree
grinning at the world.
The one of Mum and Dad,
his arm slung easily around her waist,
and the long fingers of her hands
clasped tightly together at his hip.
Before I leave,
I go to the wardrobe,
open the door,
and run my hands
along the delicate fabric
of Mum's purple dress.
I can almost smell her perfume.
I put my arms around her dress
and press my face close.
I hug Mum's dress,

with my eyes closed.
I whisper into the warm fabric
for one last time,
then I leave
my father's room.

REFLECTION

Finches, silver-eyes,
and sparrows
dart among the willows
as a breeze plays
across Pearce Swamp.
I sit on a log
and look at my
imperfect reflection:
hair too messy,
nose too long,
ears too wide,
and eyes . . .
eyes like Mum's.
I look hard for my dad.
In my hands?
My feet?
The way I walk?
Somewhere,
there must be Dad.

A noise.
Johnny Barlow stands
on the opposite bank.
We stare at each other
for minutes,

hours,

forever,

with nothing between us

but the water,

my reflection,

and Linda's ghost.

Johnny turns and walks back

into the forest.

I dip my hands into the clear water

and wipe my face.

I reach into my pocket

for Miss Spencer's locket

with a school photo

of Linda inside.

I place the chain

around the cross.

I leave Linda

for the visitor

who's circling the swamp now,

on his way . . .

PERFECT SILENCE

I walk home.
As I open the gate
I see, clearly now,
which part of me
is my dad's.
The part inside;
the good part.
The part that knows
Johnny Barlow,
Linda,
the ring,
the white cross,
the mystery of the '62 flood,
are all safe
and cherished
deep within.

I close the gate,
climb the stairs
and sit on the top rung,
waiting for Dad
and Keith to come home
in the perfect silence
of the afternoon.

HAPPINESS

I cut the last slice
of watermelon
three ways.
Keith takes bite after bite
without stopping.
The juice tracks
down his chin
in a constant stream.
I start from the middle,
one deliberate bite at a time—
the tingle of each sugar crunch.
Dad watches Keith,
turns to me,
winks,
remembers the slice
in his good hand
and takes a slow
generous bite.